Roses and Thorns

Priyanshi Vora

BookLeaf Publishing

Presentation by *BookLeaf Publishing*

Web: www.bookleafpub.com

E-mail: info@bookleafpub.com

ISBN: 9789358316728

First edition 2023

ACKNOWLEDGEMENT

I'm deeply thankful to my family and friends for their constant encouragement and support. I'm immensely grateful to my sister for constructive discussions and feedback.

I would like to extend my appreciation to BookLeaf Publishing for bringing my book to life.

My heartfelt gratitude to the readers of this book for your support and engagement.

Without the support and involvement of all these individuals, this book would not have been possible. Thank you all for your time and invaluable contributions.

Echoes of Yesterday's Love

Never anticipated this end,
our broken hearts, I thought we could mend.
Came unprepared for our last meeting,
with chaotic thoughts and wild feelings.

Our hopeless eyes locking each other,
no words could make this better.
We let the silence speak as we parted our ways,
but mentally stuck in our "together" days.

When the radio plays our favorite song,
or when I catch a whiff of your cologne,
my heart still skips a beat,
encapsulated in time - our love, once so sweet.

Feels like only yesterday that our budding
friendship,
was rooted and fostered to grow into a blossom
of love.
Now all that's left are dried up petals,
crumbling into dust.

Maybe we weren't meant to be,
maybe it wasn't our time,
maybe in a parallel universe,
you are still mine and I am forever yours.

Don't Want to Wake Up

I feel the warmth of sunshine kissing my skin,
soaking in the pain and grief that I hold within,
I feel the soft sand between my toes,
hugging and comforting my tired soles.

Against the backdrop of endless blue of the sea,
Is it really you that I see?
Have my prayers finally been answered?
"Dad, I'm here!", towards you, I advance.

Tears roll down my face,
as you wrap me in the warmth of your embrace,
broken pieces of me gluing back together,
I feel safe as a tortoise under its shell, here.

Behind you, birds soar above the sea waters,
palm trees dance to the tune of the winds
offshore,
like an old-fashioned camera, I remain still,
capturing this moment, so tranquil.

"My child, I'm glad you are here,
I'm happy and at peace,
I know no pain, hate and grief.
You must now return though,

I'll continue watching you,
from the heavenly skies of blue."

Then, my eyes flutter open, adjusting to the
morning light.

Two Homes

5

Waved goodbye to my family,
as I walked towards the airline security.
Excited to follow my dreams,
while questioning if I'll ever fit in.

Landed in the evening,
the fear of not finding a new home, seeped in.
Strange faces and languages I'd never known,
stepped into a world I now call my own.

Though initial days were a blur,
soon I learnt to embrace the unfamiliar.
Using the contrasts to widen my knowledge,
I'll imbibe the new culture, I pledged.

There are times when I miss my family,
the luxury of hugging my mom when I feel
crappy,
or charging into my sister's room when I'm
happy.
I miss the beautiful skies,
and the joyful festivities of my native country.

It's not all unicorns and rainbows,
this journey has its roses and thorns,

my heart now split between two lands,
never complete without the other, like a pair of
hands.

Forever Linked

Flicking through the creased pages of the photo
album,
I walk down our memory lane, finding solace
and calm.
From talking in codes to speaking with our eyes,
from arguing over the last bite of cake, to
laughing till sunrise,
our story of childhood and friendship unwinds.

I recall the days when you'd tag along,
I told you bedtime tales, your joy so profound.
When you won your first prize at school, my
happiness magnified,
now, watching you evolve into a young
confident woman,
my heart bursts with pride.

Shared things oh so many,
yet opposites in numerous ways.
While I'm quiet, you are loud,
while I'm shy, you are bold,
good times or bad, together we've faced it all.

Like a father I protected you,
like a mother I took care of you.

Then, came a time when our roles swapped,
you nurtured my broken heart,
and your light showed me the path in the dark.

Now, there is no elder or younger,
no naive or wiser,
no leader or a follower.
Shiny weeks or rainy days,
we walk hand in hand, come what may.

Paradise

He removes his radio from the bag,
her cheeks turn red as he takes her hand.
The chirping of crickets and the sweet chorus of
birds,
adding their own notes to the melodious song.

His hands on her slender waist,
they move to the rhythm of the beat.
Locked in each other's eyes,
dancing against the perfect palette of yellows
and reds.

From the calmness of its core,
to the ripples that danced on the top,
the lake meets the sun with such grace,
as if the two were enchanted by their dance.

His fingers meet hers', a tender touch,
pulling her even closer, he sees her blush,
gazing into her glistening emerald eyes,
he finds himself lost in her beautiful smile.

Everything around him blurs,
and it's just him and her,
a haven of bliss where his troubles are erased,

an ethereal sanctuary, a paradise indeed.

Liberated Wings

Amidst the seething chaos in her head,
she found her peace by the water ahead,
gently stepping foot into the cold stream,
the current carried away her unutterable grief.

Water gradually beginning to hug her,
giving her the warmth, she had craved since
forever,
Oh, how it held her closer,
than anybody would ever.

The tears have dried,
but her eyes still wet,
screaming from within,
she lets go of her hand's grip.

Her lips stop mid-sentence,
her final question left unanswered,
winds carry away this weight of her sorrow,
while she pushes her way through, under the
weeping willow.

Her long messy braid unwinding,
her dirty lace tangled in a withered branch, torn,
loosening her silver gown.

Bedded in the gurgling stream,
she finally felt free.

Motherhood

Round nose and cherubic cheeks,
tiny fingers held in a grasp so meek.
From faint flutters to kicks and turns so bold,
he had once taken up all the space in her womb.

When the world is rocked to sleep,
he keeps her awake while he weeps.
Working double shifts to make ends meet,
a vicious cycle she repeats.

A milk bottle, a stroller and diaper bags,
distressed face and weary eyes,
often paranoid and all on her own,
she struggles all alone.

A protector, shielding him from harm,
a nurturer, loving and showering him with care,
a mother, a caregiver and a provider,
but more than all, she is a superhero without a
cape.

Nine to Five

Slow moving traffic jam,
podcast on Spotify, yeah! That's my jam.

Waiting in congestion, a frustrating urge,
work commute is the absolute worst.

It's nine am, I'm badged in,
but first, a quick visit to the coffee machine.

Seated at the desk, I better check my emails,
requests and inquiries, deadlines to meet.

A pending presentation, an unfinished report,
I hope the meeting gets postponed.

Enters she, my work bestie,
a friendly face amidst the office's sea.

A pop up on the screen grabs my attention,
an unplanned meeting, I nod and smile until it's
done.

Its noon, time for a salad bowl and crunchy
chickpeas,
and then back to my pending duties.

So many errors in red,
so many comments to address.

Focus mode on,
chop-chop got to grind this down.

Three hours pass, its five pm,
I log off from the digital realm.

Time to unwind and recharge,
for tomorrow will come with new demands.

Aging Gracefully

Wrinkles and fine lines,
a roadmap of her times.
Gray hair and crepey skin,
a touch of wisdom and sophistication,
rocking the silver fox impression.

Hearing loss and decreasing visual acuity,
playing the game of "Guess who?" in reality.
Unclear sounds and muffled voices,
asking "what did you say?" a few extra times,
mistaken identities and unexpected surprises,
making her life even more interesting.

Opening jars and lifting grocery bags,
each day a new struggle at hand.
No more limber and agile,
but can reach the remote control from the sofa,
just fine.

Betrayed by her advancing age,
failed by her own memory,
but, underneath this frazzled shell,
is a spirit that never quells.

Touchstone Bond

Building sand beach forts,
riding bicycles on neighborhood roads,
new experiences and innocent adventures,
joy and spontaneity, we shared together.

Secrets under a blanket den,
hopes and promises we held,
fantasy worlds and dream visions,
navigating a world of our imaginations.

Loyalty, support and trust,
pillars of our enduring friendship,
enriching our lives in myriad of ways,
through both cheerful and challenging days.

Our deep understanding transcending time,
my companion in need, you are my prime,
twenty years now, our friendship still strong,
can hardly believe it has been this long.

With you,
I'm ported into a time capsule,
your warmth providing constancy and
belonging,
in this world that's continually changing.

The Beginning or the End?

Pressed shirt and a jacket of leather,
an attire well put together.

Frequent stares at his watch,
occasional sips from the glass of scotch,
eagerness like tingling curves,
desperate attempts to quell those lingering
nerves.

To keep busy, he flips through the menu,
going through the contents anew.

A smile brightens his face,
as he finally spots his date,
awkward handshakes and greetings,
sweaty palms and flushed faces.

Fidgeting, she unfolds her napkin into a tangled
mess,
fumbling, he struggles with his utensils.

Will the chocolate mousse be their ice breaker?
or will this be one of the awkward dates to
remember?

Will this lead to the beginning of something
new?
or will this rendezvous vanish into the blue?

Magic in the Mundane

An array of colorful dried petals,
the aroma of sweet berries and rose, settles,
pouring hot water over the tea blend,
an enchanting ritual trends.

Like pixie dust, awakening dreams,
a pinch of salt, enhances flavors,
simmering sauces and sprinkling spices, you see,
cooking becomes a magical decree.

Two white t-shirts, now dried,
neatly folded, side by side,
the humble chore of folding laundry,
a cadence of tranquility.

Vibrant and bustling streets, a daily commute,
weaving through the throng, a monotonous
pursuit,
amidst the chaos, laughter and conversations
compound,
finding comfort in the rhythm of the crowd.

Water drops from heaven,
cleansing our souls; our sins forgiven,
rain falling on the ground,

a pitter-patter melody in the mundane.

From dusty corners to shining floors,
the act of cleaning, where beauty takes hold.
Open your hearts and dive deep inside,
for you will see, in the ordinary, magic resides.

Phoenix's Dance

Loved unconditionally, no reservations,
trusted deeply without hesitation,
hopeful eyes, undying determination,
she gave it all without any expectations.

Love's journey, not always kind,
pain of disappointment pierced her inside,
betrayal stung her from behind,
trials and afflictions, her sorrows amplified.

Broken promises, her heart at stake,
lingering within, a pain she can't shake,
yet through the darkness a strength awakes,
to give life another shot and learn from past
mistakes.

Like a phoenix, she rose from the ashes of
deceit,
defying the odds, listening to her heartbeats,
breaking the chains of the past with great might,
a world of strength and resiliency, she ignites.

Love's Unbalanced Scale

You needed your alone time,
but I wanted us to share the nights,
always exhausted, you'd no time for dinner
dates,
but with you, I longed to stargaze.

I'd hoped that someday,
you will willingly ask about my day,
that you will take me somewhere,
to show me how much you care.

Now, tired of watering our dead roses,
yearning for your love, in vain,
tired of loving again and again,
my broken heart longs for a mend.

Our love's flame no longer bright,
for you were never really mine,
the bond we shared, destined to not grow,
I held onto moments that were only borrowed.

The only option left to take,
is to let go of you for my own sake,
for your lips are sore from kissing another love,

for all your favorite songs have been sung to
another heart.

Lost and Found

"Honey, where are the car keys?"
I stare at the empty key holder, what a tease!
Michael emerges from the rear,
"Well, didn't you hang it there?"

Irritated and confused,
I desperately search my pockets and purse.
Already late for the party,
hoping I find the damn keys.

An hour of retracing my steps,
from the closet to the bathroom and next.
Turning upside down,
whatever my eyes land on.

My 4-year-old and my dog stare at me,
did they hide the keys?
Their expressions so cryptic,
are they clueless or mocking me?

In the shoes,
between the seat cushions,
and under the couch,
the keys were nowhere to be found.

Too late for the party now,
I changed into my nightgown.
Hungry, I open the fridge and see my car keys,
stuck between spring rolls and frozen beans!

Imperfectly Perfect

In a delicate masterpiece of white lace,
she walks down the aisle with elegance and
grace.
Momentarily losing her control, she almost slips,
but soon regains her balance and grip.

Honest and heartfelt vows are exchanged,
but in the middle of an "I do", the groom
sneezed,
letting out an "achoo" instead.

In a mix up of boxes,
the wrong ring is handed,
all eyes on the best man,
rectifying his mistake, with trembling hands.

Adorned with flowers, tall and grand,
the cake was cut hand in hand,
but soon the layers start to slide south,
like a castle of sand, the cake topples down.

Despite the mishaps and chaos,
with smiles and laughter, the couple embraced it
all,

for it's not the perfect "I do's" or the ring or the
cake,
but what matters is the love that they share.

Unexpected Reunion

Across the room, beside the fireplace,
my eyes land on a familiar face.
Seeing you again after all this time,
awakened the feelings that were buried deep
inside.

Unspoken words and awkward silence,
still haunted by the echoes of the past.
Time and distance have taken their toll,
leaving us with fragments of our broken love.

Like I've been put on a rollercoaster ride,
emotions and memories resurface, flooding my
heart and mind.
Meeting you again is bittersweet,
but I must now set my lingering feelings free.

Hopefully, in this reunion we find a closure,
and bid farewell to what hurt us before.
Let the moments that we shared be our guiding
force,
towards a lasting love that we both deserve.

Dare to Descent

Release of liability form handed to me,
"Is it really safe?", the thought scared me.
With a racing heart and trembling hands,
I sign the papers, unsure of the next.

Things to do and not to do,
the process, they guide us through,
unable to absorb any of it,
I put on my safety suit, as I panic.

Off to the mountain in a jeep,
"Is it too late to play sick?"
A quick scan of my surroundings,
happy faces and excited spirits.

Feeling weak in my knees,
I need some time to breathe.
Terrified, I stand last in the line,
buying time as much as I can.

Most dreaded, my turn has come,
"Don't worry, it will be fun!",
he said with a big smile,
as he hooked me to the zip line.

Through canopies of green,
and the world below me,
I glide with grace,
in a thrilling chase.

Feeling the adrenaline rush as I zip through,
with every second my confidence grew.
As I reach the bottom, I let out a triumph shout,
proud to have conquered my fear and doubts.

Blessed

My birth mother, nurturing and gentle,
our enduring bond, oh! so special.
Through sleepless nights and highs and lows,
her love and strength, a guiding force.

Then, my elder aunt who embraced me as her
own,
showering kindness and support when I feel
alone.
With open arms and a listening ear,
she brings me warmth through smiles and tears.

Next, my grandmother, wise and kind,
who believed in me when no one did.
Warm hugs and lots of kisses - no discounts,
her selfless love knew no bounds.

Then, my younger aunt, supportive and patient,
always there for me without hesitation.
Through every challenge, by my side,
she guides me through life's turbulent tide.

Blessed with four mothers,
through life's maze, my guiding stars.
Each unique, with a heart so pure,

together they've shaped me, heart and soul.

33

Furry Friend

Golden and cream,
furry and thick,
oh, how we instantly clicked.

Welcoming strangers with open paws,
your friendliness knows no bounds.
Wagging your tail and licking cheeks,
with abundance of love, you meet and greet.

The pain of my first heartache,
the joy on my graduation day,
through all my ups and downs,
in you, a loyal companion I have found.

But, oh the trouble that you create,
chewing on anything and everything, a constant
headache.
From clothes to carpets and furniture,
a flurry of fur, everywhere I turn.

Sticking your head outside the car's window,
without worrying about tomorrow,
feeling the breeze against your fur,
you find happiness in simple pleasures.

To savor each day and night,
you taught me how to embrace life.
Cozy snuggles and exuberant greetings,
you've loved me without any conditions.

Metamorphosis

Childhood's innocence and eyes full of dreams,
a world where imagination streams.
Looking up to adults with awe and admiration,
yearning for adulthood, to make our own
decisions.

Come the youth years, spreading our wings,
guided with passion, we follow our dreams.
Navigating our way through boundless
possibilities,
we carve out our paths from life's ever-changing
lanes.

Lessons learnt through triumph and loss,
with passing time, age takes a toll.
Sailing through the currents with unwavering
strength,
we realize the weight of responsibilities and
burdens.

Strained with worries and despair,
yearning for the innocence we used to share.
Once so carefree and light,
a time, we can't rewind.

From naive beginnings to seasoned souls,
we learn and grow to reach our goals,
like a caterpillar, small and fragile,
to a butterfly, vibrant and bright.

Life's journey, always taking us forward,
shaping our character, where maturity blossoms.
For in this circle of life, we find our true worth,
so let's embrace each chapter with open hearts.